Blood Diamonds

- Blood Diamonds 2
- Diamond in the Rough 4
- Digging for Diamonds 8
- Tracing the Path 14
- The Diamond Industry Reacts 18
- The Kimberley Process 22
- Blood Diamonds Today 24

Blood Diamonds

CLARIFY
proclaims
rugged
innocuous-looking
atrocities
civilians
harrowing

A diamond is forever, or so the television advertisement proclaims, with an orchestra playing in the background. The silhouette of a man appears onscreen and slips towards the shadow of a woman. They are only faceless shapes, because the object in the man's hand is what matters most. He drops to one knee and flips open a small box, revealing a brilliant diamond ring. The music swells as the camera zooms in on the gem – shimmering, as if on fire from within. The camera inspects each gleaming facet, polished to perfection. This exquisite gem, the advertisement tells us, represents the promise of enduring love and loyalty.

And yet, if we could trace the diamond's path from the time it was taken from the earth, rugged and dull, to the time it found a home on the woman's ring finger, we might uncover a very different story.

If these innocuous-looking gems could talk, many would tell tales not of love but of unfathomable violence and destruction – of families torn apart and innocent lives taken, all in the name of profits. Many of the diamonds glinting on fingers, wrists and necklines today are conflict diamonds, also known as blood diamonds.

READER RESPONSE
How did the introduction evoke interest in the topic? Do you think the author hooked in the reader successfully? Why/why not?

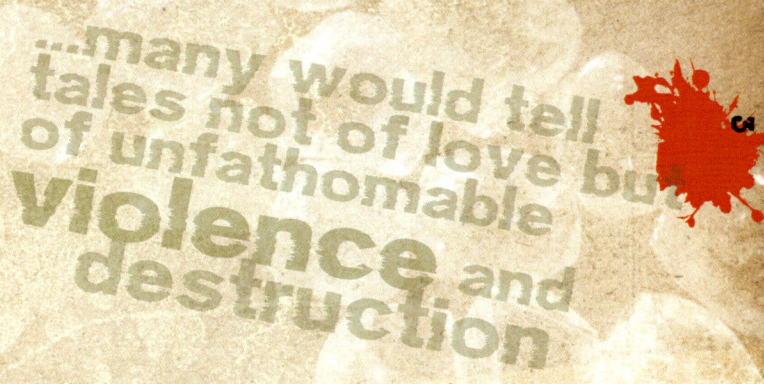

...many would tell tales not of love but of unfathomable **violence** and **destruction**

By definition, blood diamonds are those that have been used to fuel conflict and civil war. Throughout the 1990s and early 21st century, rebel forces in African nations such as Sierra Leone, Angola and the Democratic Republic of the the Congo (DRC) inflicted untold atrocities on opponents and civilians with weapons funded by diamond sales. Though these civil wars ended shortly after the turn of the century, all three countries and their neighbours are still reeling from the effects. And blood diamonds remain a problem in a few African nations, such as Côte d'Ivoire (formerly Ivory Coast).

A diamond's journey from the Earth's mantle to a little velvet box can be a harrowing one, driven by people whose desire for profit far outweighs their concern for human lives and rights. It's a journey that, if recounted to the woman accepting the stone, might make her think twice before slipping it onto her finger

AUTHOR PURPOSE
Why do you think the author might have written this book?

Diamond in the Rough

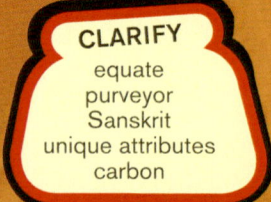

CLARIFY
equate
purveyor
Sanskrit
unique attributes
carbon

Those in Western society who have come to equate diamonds with love are not the first to find symbolism in these precious gems. In fact, offering a diamond as a token of love is only a recent tradition in the gem's long history. It has also represented, among many other things, strength and purity, as well as acting as a purveyor of good luck and a repellent for evil.

The word "diamond" comes from the Greek word "adamao", which translates as "I tame" or "I subdue". In India, where diamond mining first originated as far back as the fourth century BC, the gem's Sanskrit name meant "Thunderbolt, Indra's Weapon" (Indra was a warrior god). According to the ancient Hindus, a person who wore a pure diamond would experience happiness and prosperity and would be protected from dangers such as serpents, fire and poison.

The hardness of different compounds measured on the Mohs scale of mineral hardness

a pencil lead	gypsum	a fingernail	calcite	apatite	a knife blade	feldspar	quartz	topaz	diamond
1	2	2.5	3	5	5.5	6	7	8	10

Softest — Hardest

The diamond earned such a reputation thanks to a few unique attributes: its hardness and what gem experts call its "brilliance" and "fire". With a crystal structure made up entirely of carbon in its most concentrated form, the diamond is the hardest known surface on Earth, with the highest rating on the Mohs hardness scale. **Diamonds are so hard, in fact, that they can only be scratched by other diamonds.** This trait makes them a valuable abrasive, used to cut metal and other stones.

The chemical element of a diamond

6
12.001
C
Carbon

Atomic number
Atomic weight
Symbol of element
Name of element

RESEARCH
What do you know about the Mohs hardness scale? Research where this scale originated and how it is used.

token of love
strength
purity
diamonds

QUESTION GENERATE
What questions do you have about this information?

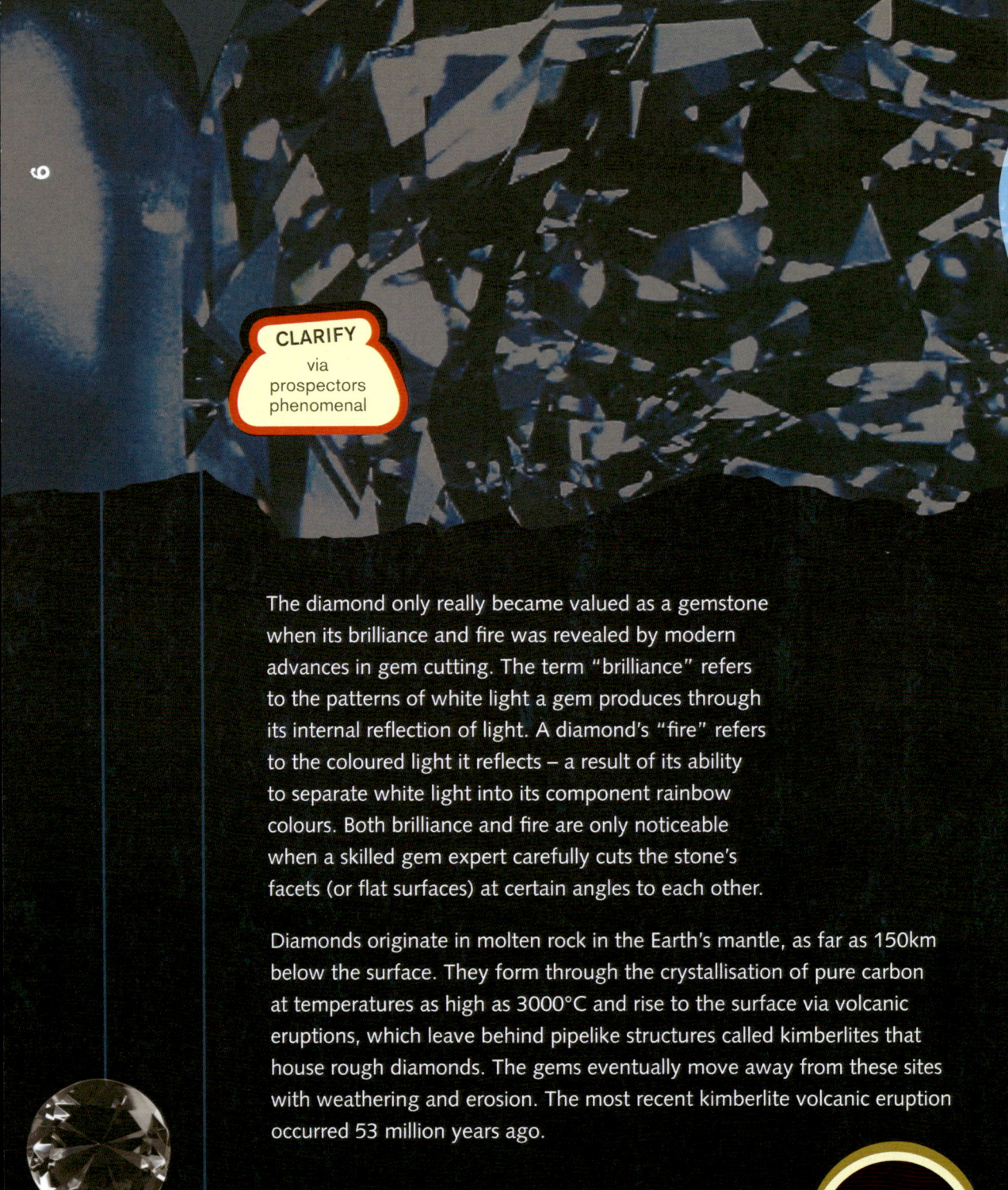

CLARIFY
via
prospectors
phenomenal

The diamond only really became valued as a gemstone when its brilliance and fire was revealed by modern advances in gem cutting. The term "brilliance" refers to the patterns of white light a gem produces through its internal reflection of light. A diamond's "fire" refers to the coloured light it reflects – a result of its ability to separate white light into its component rainbow colours. Both brilliance and fire are only noticeable when a skilled gem expert carefully cuts the stone's facets (or flat surfaces) at certain angles to each other.

Diamonds originate in molten rock in the Earth's mantle, as far as 150km below the surface. They form through the crystallisation of pure carbon at temperatures as high as 3000°C and rise to the surface via volcanic eruptions, which leave behind pipelike structures called kimberlites that house rough diamonds. The gems eventually move away from these sites with weathering and erosion. The most recent kimberlite volcanic eruption occurred 53 million years ago.

What do you think a report on the journey of a diamond from mine to consumer will include?

PREDICT

Location of diamond-mining countries – 2009

CANADA, UNITED STATES OF AMERICA, GUYANA, VENEZUELA, BRAZIL, IVORY COAST, GUINEA, SIERRA LEONE, LIBERIA, GHANA, ANGOLA, BOTSWANA, NAMIBIA, SOUTH AFRICA, LESOTHO, RUSSIAN FEDERATION, CHINA, INDIA, DEMOCRATIC REPUBLIC OF CONGO, TANZANIA, ZIMBABWE, INDONESIA, AUSTRALIA

SUPPOSITION
A supposition is an idea or opinion that is formed on the basis of limited evidence, rather than real proof. Find any examples?

...the diamonds' journey has only just begun

The diamond only really became valued as a gemstone when modern advances in gem cutting revealed its brilliance and fire. **Though they've come a long way already, travelling incredible distances under phenomenal pressure, the diamonds' journey has only just begun.**

Digging for Diamonds

CLARIFY
subsistence
unregulated
diamond reserves
corruption

It's a blazing hot and humid day, but the diamond diggers – standing calf-deep in a brown river, eyes glued to the gravel before them – don't seem to notice the heat. A few dozen of them crowd this alluvial diamond mine in the West African country of Sierra Leone. Alluvial diamonds are those that have been transported by water from their kimberlite sources over millions of years, ending up in riverbeds and on shorelines or ocean floors. The men who spend countless hours sifting through gravel with simple sieves and pans are called "artisanal" miners or diggers, meaning they do their business on a subsistence level, with simple tools. Artisanal diggers are usually unlicensed and unregulated by the larger mining industry. It's estimated that there are more than a million such diggers in Africa.

ISSUES
What issues are raised by the use of child labour in diamond mines?

Artisanal miners lead hard, dangerous and unhealthy lives, usually earning no more than a dollar a day for the few gems they find and sell to diamond dealers.

The artisanal mining industry has no health and safety regulations, no laws to protect the environment and no rules to prevent child labour in the mines. Children often work alongside their fathers, knee-deep in water and mud.

INFERENCE
What inferences can you make about why artisanal miners usually earn no more than a dollar a day for their work?

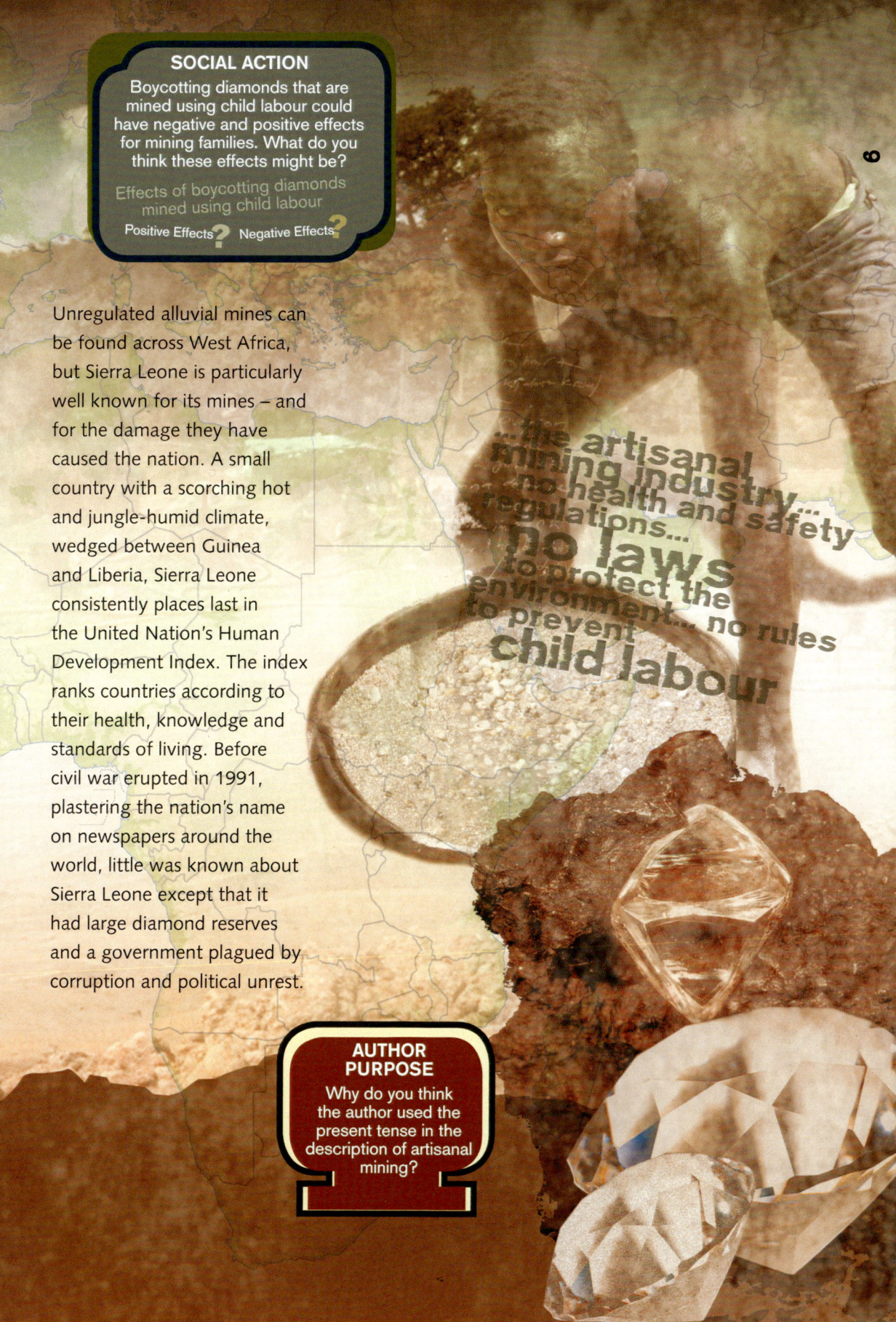

SOCIAL ACTION

Boycotting diamonds that are mined using child labour could have negative and positive effects for mining families. What do you think these effects might be?

Effects of boycotting diamonds mined using child labour

Positive Effects? Negative Effects?

...the artisanal mining industry... no health and safety regulations... no laws to protect the environment... no rules to prevent child labour

Unregulated alluvial mines can be found across West Africa, but Sierra Leone is particularly well known for its mines – and for the damage they have caused the nation. A small country with a scorching hot and jungle-humid climate, wedged between Guinea and Liberia, Sierra Leone consistently places last in the United Nation's Human Development Index. The index ranks countries according to their health, knowledge and standards of living. Before civil war erupted in 1991, plastering the nation's name on newspapers around the world, little was known about Sierra Leone except that it had large diamond reserves and a government plagued by corruption and political unrest.

AUTHOR PURPOSE

Why do you think the author used the present tense in the description of artisanal mining?

CLARIFY
grave difference
civil war
signature brand
ultimate reminders

Ten to 15 years ago, you would have seen something similar to this: wiry men hunched over sieves, their feet sinking into the riverbed. Except there would have been one grave difference: a gang of men watching from the shore, armed with rifles, ready to assault the diggers if their work slowed or stopped. They would be ready to catch them if they tried to run away; ready to kill them if they attempted to pocket a diamond for themselves.

These armed guards were part of the Revolutionary United Front (RUF), the main rebel group driving Sierra Leone's decade-long civil war. They fought government armies and West African peacekeepers for control of the country's diamond mines, selling the gems to arm themselves with Kalashnikov rifles and AK-47s. The diamond diggers were mainly villagers they had kidnapped and forced to dig. Rarely did the RUF actually pay the diggers, though sometimes they were allowed to keep the lowest value gems they uncovered.

BEYOND THE TEXT
What comparisons can you make between the forced labour used by the RUF and other examples of forced labour?

VISUAL FEATURES
What impact do the visual features (design and images) have on you? What sub-messages are conveyed by the images?

The RUF had no regard for human lives and respected no rights or boundaries. In fact, much of its army consisted of drugged-up teenagers kidnapped from local villages. The RUF's war was marked by gruesome torture, rape and murder. Its signature brand of violence was amputation. After Sierra Leone's president, Ahmad Tejan Kabbah, pleaded in 1996 for civilians to "join hands" in peace, the RUF began to cut off people's hands randomly and leave them on the steps of the presidential palace. **Today, tens of thousands of Sierra Leoneans are living with severed limbs... the ultimate reminders of the violence.**

The rest of the world made feeble attempts to stop the war, with little success. It raged on, leaving more than 75,000 people dead and thousands more tortured. Meanwhile, the RUF mined up to $125 million worth of diamonds every year.

EMOTIONAL APPEAL
Has the author used emotional appeal to manipulate your feelings about the RUF or stuck to reporting the facts? What do you think?

"...a gang of armed with rifles assault the diggers... ready to catch them if they tried to run away... ready to kill them"

> **CLARIFY**
> played out
> insurgent
> tenuous
> demobilisation
> perilous

Similar diamond-fuelled conflicts – although perhaps not so graphic – were also played out elsewhere in Africa. From 1961 to 2002, 500,000 people lost their lives in a civil war led by the Angolan rebel political group UNITA, which controlled 60 to 70 per cent of the country's diamonds. Another war raged in the Democratic Republic of the Congo from 1998 to 2003, this time between insurgent groups competing for control of diamond-rich areas in the north-east.

These three wars have given way to tenuous peace. In Sierra Leone, the United Nations (UN) eventually established a costly peacekeeping mission and, after a long and violent demobilisation process, the government settled down to rebuild a battered nation. As is often the case with Third World conflict, the international community was slow to pay attention to the atrocities, which were far removed from stable Western societies. (It didn't help that journalists were evacuated from Sierra Leone because of the perilous conditions, so images and information about what was happening were unavailable to the public.)

> **READER RESPONSE**
> Have your feelings about diamonds changed because of the information in this book? Why/why not?

The effects of civil war reached far beyond these countries' borders. And the diamonds that funded years of torture were already halfway around the world, settling onto the fingers and wrists of people who could not have imagined the suffering they had caused.

INFERENCE

"…the international community was slow to pay attention to the atrocities, which were far removed from stable Western societies."

What inferences can you make about why the international community was slow to respond to the atrocities committed in Sierra Leone?

Link between diamonds and human rights abuses in some African countries

Diamond-producing Country	Human Rights Abuses
Angola	Abuse, disappearances, torture and killing of people
Botswana	Excessive force used by police during the interrogation of "suspects"
Central African Republic	Torture, beatings, kidnappings, killing and rape of people by security forces and armed groups. Abuse of "suspects" and prisoners by security forces
Congo Brazzaville	Mob violence, including the killing of suspected criminals; security force beatings, physical abuse of detainees, rapes and looting. Corruption, theft and bribery, including the extortion of innocent people and international NGO workers
Democratic Republic of the Congo	Abuse, torture, rape and killing of people by security forces and armed groups operating outside of government control
Ghana	Excessive force used by police which resulted in beatings, deaths, vigilante justice and politically/ethnically motivated violence
Guinea	Beatings, abuse and killing of innocent people by security forces

…**the effects of civil war reached far beyond these countries' borders**

ISSUES

What issues are raised when journalists are prevented from reporting events in war zones?

Tracing the Path

CLARIFY

legitimate
procured
damning

In Sierra Leone, there is a legitimate system through which diamonds ought to travel when leaving the country. Exporters should purchase mining and export licences from the government, allowing them to employ licensed diggers and buyers. Once these licences are procured, exporters are supposed to bring their diamonds to Freetown, the country's capital, where they can be valued, taxed and given a certificate saying they originated in Sierra Leone. The exporter can then leave the country with the gems and sell them elsewhere.

...where there are diamonds there are usually diamond smugglers

OPINION
What is your opinion of countries such as Guinea and Liberia and the role they played in receiving diamonds from Sierra Leone?

Unfortunately, the system doesn't always work that way. Where there are diamonds, there are usually diamond smugglers. During Sierra Leone's decade of terror, the RUF would take its gems to neighbouring countries, such as Guinea and Liberia, in order to avoid export taxes and, of course, the damning label "blood diamonds". There the RUF would trade them for rice, fuel or weapons.

Guinea and Liberia had no restrictions or certification requirements and were even known to hand out certificates saying that the gems came from their countries rather than Sierra Leone. This explains why diamonds continued to enter the diamond trade even after the UN banned the sale of all diamonds from Sierra Leone in May 2000.

VISUAL FEATURES
How do the visual features reference, or suggest, the underworld environment of the diamond smuggler?

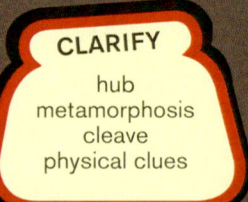

CLARIFY
hub
metamorphosis
cleave
physical clues

It also partly explains why it is virtually impossible to trace the origins of a diamond. Until quite recently, the Diamond High Council in Antwerp, Belgium (a hub for the diamond trade), recorded the last country to ship the gems as the country of origin for the diamonds cut and polished in Antwerp. Diamonds could therefore pass from Sierra Leone to Liberia to Belgium, and the diamond capital of Europe would view them as non-conflict gems.

SYMBOLISM
Why has the author used the term "metamorphosis"? Is this a symbolic reference? Why/why not?

In Antwerp, and in cities in Israel, Thailand, India, South Africa and the US, diamonds begin their metamorphosis from rough stones to perfect jewels – increasing in price every time they change hands. First they are refined and sorted by type and quality. During this process, diamonds from all over the world get mixed together, then offered for sale to diamond cutters, who analyse how best to cleave each gem.

VISUAL FEATURES
How might you visually interpret the textual information about the processing of a diamond?

The diamond continues its journey from the setters, who mount it as jewellery, to finishers and quality analysers, before it ends up in the hands of the person who receives it as a precious, timeless gift. At this point, it is impossible to determine a diamond's origins. Once polished and cut, the stone bears no physical clues to indicate its original home.

...once polished and cut, the stone bears no physical clues to indicate its original home

AUTHOR MESSAGE
What underlying message does the author have for people who view diamonds as "a precious, timeless gift"?

QUESTION
Should traders such as the Diamond High Council in Antwerp show more responsibility in tracking the origin of the diamonds they handle? Why/why not?

The Diamond Industry Reacts

CLARIFY
valid
indifference
dubious origins
colossal
financial clout

The fighting in Sierra Leone, Angola and the DRC had been going on for several years before the international community decided that the situation required its intervention. **The diamond industry, which is dependent on the immense number of gems it receives from these countries every year, was initially reluctant to change its ways.** In fact, the industry only began to worry about blood diamonds when two non-profit organisations, Global Witness and Partnership Africa Canada (PAC), came up with a publicity campaign that no one could ignore.

FACT OR OPINION

"The industry's worries were probably fuelled more by a fear of plummeting sales than concern for the welfare of African war victims."

Fact or opinion? What do you think?

The industry's worries were probably fuelled more by a fear of plummeting sales than concern for the welfare of African war victims. But their fears were valid. As Global Witness and PAC produced graphic reports about the RUF's actions and the diamond industry's indifference, many consumers began to question the sources of the diamonds they were buying and even to refuse to buy those with dubious origins.

Still, changing a powerful industry is no easy feat, particularly when that industry is dominated by a few colossal companies. Thanks to their sheer size and financial clout, these companies can control the sales of an entire industry. The De Beers Group is a cartel – a group of firms designed to limit competition and/or fix prices – that mines half of the world's annual diamond output and controls up to 80 per cent of diamond sales through its Central Selling Organisation.

That organisation buys and stocks diamonds from other suppliers to keep availability low and prices high. **It has shaped the face of the diamond industry we know today.**

...consumers began to question the sources of the diamonds they were buying and even to refuse to buy those with dubious origins

READING BETWEEN THE LINES
What potential do you think the consumer has to change the way the diamond industry operates?

CLARIFY
intrinsic value
entity
synonymous
crucial
fiancés
industry executives

...a diamond is forever

Until the late 19th century, diamonds had only been found in remote corners of Brazil and India and were thought to be extremely rare. As a result, diamond sellers could ask very high prices. But, when prospectors happened upon plentiful diamond mines in South Africa in 1870, the industry realised that diamonds were in fact so common, they had little intrinsic value. **The major diamond investors of the time hatched a plan to create a single powerful entity that could control diamond production and prices – De Beers.** It soon proved to be the most successful cartel in history, thanks to a scheme to control demand as well as supply.

In the 1940s, De Beers hired a marketing firm to help convince Americans that diamonds were the world's most desirable gem (the idea had never quite caught on in Europe). They targeted young men and women, instilling the belief that diamonds were synonymous with – and a crucial part of – romance. To do this, they enlisted the media and celebrities, arranging for movie stars to wear diamonds before the camera.

ANALYSIS
In what way did De Beers use emotional appeal to manipulate its targeted audience? Do you think the post-war timing of the campaign was a significant factor in its success? Why/why not?

They even arranged for lecturers to visit high schools throughout the country, teaching young women to demand diamonds from their future fiancés.

In 1947, a copywriter for the marketing agency came up with the slogan "A diamond is forever". As De Beers' motto, it has become one of the most successful slogans in history. In the 1960s, the cartel took this marketing scheme to the rest of the world, convincing countries such as Brazil and Japan that they ought to live up to Western standards and demand diamonds as symbols of love.

Throughout the 1990s, De Beers continued to purchase diamonds from Angola, Sierra Leone and other African conflict zones, showing little inclination to change its ways. But even an industry heavyweight is not above consumer pressure. The public's demand to know where its diamonds came from, coupled with the post-September 11, 2001 discovery that the infamous Al Qaeda also funded its activities with conflict diamonds, left De Beers and other corporations with no choice but to join the conflict-free diamond movement. Fortunately, a group of organisations, governments and industry executives made it simple for the cartel to look as though it had turned a new leaf. All it had to do was sign up to the Kimberley Process.

> **ISSUES**
> "[De Beers] even arranged for lecturers to visit high schools throughout the country, teaching young women to demand diamonds from their future fiancés."
> What issues does this advertising strategy raise for you?

The Kimberley Process

CLARIFY
controversial
officially launched
financial backing

In May 2000, the major names in the diamond industry, along with the governments of diamond-producing countries, met in Kimberley, South Africa. In response to international pressure from concerned non-profit organisations and consumers, they were trying to solve the issue of conflict diamonds. Three years later, after many often controversial meetings, they officially launched the Kimberley Process Certification Scheme. This system requires governments to certify that the rough diamonds they import are conflict-free. **Forty-eight countries have joined so far; these nations may only trade diamonds with other participants.**

ANALYSIS
How could governments improve the situation in the diamond mining industry?

...governments have trouble certifying that the diamonds they export are conflict free...

However, though the Kimberley Process has been effective in uniting the diamond industry and raising awareness about blood diamonds, it has not entirely eliminated the problem. The process makes it more difficult for blood diamonds to enter the trade, but certainly not impossible. Watchful organisations such as Global Witness are calling for stronger governmental controls over countries' diamond industries.

Some governments have trouble certifying that the diamonds they export are conflict-free, also making it impossible for importing countries to certify them.

The Kimberley Process is volunteer-run and in need of more financial backing. And, though some big names in the diamond industry strongly support the scheme, many have yet to take action to track diamonds themselves.

> **READING BETWEEN THE LINES**
> Why do you think many governments are slow in introducing stronger controls over the diamond industry?

> **QUESTION**
> Do you think companies trading in diamonds should financially back the Kimberley Process Scheme? Why/Why not?

Blood Diamonds Today

CLARIFY
signatories
implement
ethical sources
narrow definition
degrades
grave issue

Fewer blood or conflict diamonds are traded globally today. But organisations such as Global Witness insist that this is mainly due to the fact that the civil wars in Sierra Leone and Angola have ended. Blood diamonds are still a known issue in parts of the DRC and Côte d'Ivoire, where diamonds from areas controlled by rebel groups are being smuggled into the legitimate trade. Global Witness warns that more diamond-fuelled wars could occur in the near future unless the Kimberley Process signatories take action and implement stronger controls.

READER RESPONSE
"[Some retailers] claim that conflict diamonds are no longer an issue because they now only account for a very small percentage of the global trade."
What personal feelings are evoked by this statement?

Though some retailers try hard to ensure that their gems come from ethical sources, others claim that conflict diamonds are no longer an issue because they now only account for a very small percentage of the global trade. But such claims are based on the Kimberley Process' narrow definition of "conflict diamonds" as diamonds from nations in an official state of civil war. Therefore, technically, state-sanctioned (or government-approved) violence can be funded by diamond sales and those gems would still be defined as conflict-free.

Approximate value of diamond production within Africa

| $3.3 billion Botswana | $1.5 billion Angola | $1.5 billion South Africa | $0.9 billion Namibia | $0.7 billion Democratic Republic of the Congo | $0.6 billion Other African nations |

Values shown in US dollars

Whether or not they're officially labelled a conflict diamond, illicit (or smuggled) diamonds still account for a significant portion of the world's diamond trade – some groups claim up to 20 per cent. **And, whether or not diamond miners have AK-47s pointed their way as they dig, they still toil in dangerous conditions, receiving very little pay for the gems they find.** The industry still employs children and degrades environments in many parts of the world. The ethics of diamond mining are still a grave issue and one the world should not ignore.

> **INFERENCE**
> What inferences can you make about the author's beliefs and purpose for writing this book? What helped you form your opinion?

...government-approved violence can be funded by diamond sales

CLARIFY
written policy
tokens

If you are a concerned consumer who wants to buy diamonds, you will have to put time and effort into researching their source.

Ask to see a diamond retailer's written policy on conflict diamonds and refuse to buy if they cannot present the relevant information. If they can, take a close look at it, making sure their definition of conflict diamonds includes issues of human rights, labour and environmental laws. Retailers should also be able to present information on the conditions of the mines and cutting/polishing facilities from which they source.

Ethical and sustainable diamonds do exist and the more consumers insist on purchasing them, the faster the diamond industry will be forced to clean up its act. Eventually, we may not have to wonder if our sparkling tokens of undying love have left an invisible trail of suffering.

QUESTION
What is meant by the phrase "to clean up its act"?

VISUAL FEATURES
How would you develop campaign materials to raise public awareness about blood diamonds?

...sparkling tokens of undying love... invisible trail of suffering

Index

alluvial diamond mines 8, 9
Angola 3, 12, 18, 21, 24
artisanal miners/diggers 8, 10
Côte d'Ivoire 3, 24
De Beers Group 19, 20, 21
Democratic Republic of the Congo (DRC) 3, 12, 18, 24
Diamond High Council 16
diamond
    advertising 2, 20-21
    certification 14, 15, 22, 23
    consumers 18, 21, 26
    cutters 6, 16, 26
    diggers 8, 10, 14
    ethics 24, 25, 26
    industry 8, 14, 16, 18-23, 26
    smugglers 15
    structure 5, 6
    symbolism 4
Global Witness 18, 23, 24
international community 12, 18
Kimberley Process 21, 22-23, 24
kimberlites 6, 8
Mohs hardness scale 4, 5
Partnership Africa Canada (PAC) 18
Revolutionary United Front (RUF) 10-11, 15, 18
Sierra Leone 3, 8, 9, 10, 11, 12, 14, 15, 16, 18, 21, 24
United Nations 9, 12, 15

READER RESPONSE
Has the information in this book challenged/changed your view of diamonds? Why/why not?

THINK ABOUT THE TEXT

MAKING CONNECTIONS — what connections can you make to the information presented in *Blood Diamonds*?

TEXT TO SELF

- Thinking about ways to support organisations that help people who are suffering in the diamond industry
- Seeing through the myths about the desirability of diamonds
- Thinking about diamonds in a new context
- Feeling let down by the media for not exposing the diamond industry
- Thinking about ways to verify a diamond's history
- Understanding how advertising creates consumer demand for diamonds
- Thinking about ways to prevent exploitation of diamond miners

TEXT TO TEXT/MEDIA

Discuss what connections you can make between this informational text and other media you have read or seen.

TEXT TO WORLD

Talk about situations in the world that might connect to elements in the text.

PLANNING AN INFORMATIONAL REPORT

1. RESEARCH

A. SELECT A TOPIC

B. BRAINSTORM THE QUESTIONS YOU NEED TO ASK

Blood Diamonds

- What is being done by the international community about violence and bad conditions in the industry?
- What are blood diamonds?
- Why do people buy diamonds?
- Where are diamonds found?
- What conditions do artisanal miners work under and what are they paid?
- What dangers are involved in digging for diamonds?
- What can people do to check the history of a diamond before purchase?
- What organisations control the mines?
- Why is violence a factor in the diamond mining industry?
- What conflicts are sparked by diamond mining?

C. USE MULTIMEDIA RESOURCES FOR YOUR INVESTIGATION

Internet, library, journals, television documentaries, encyclopedias, newspapers, interviews with experts/organisations, DVDs, magazines, research documents…

D. SKIM-READ AND TAKE NOTES
as you research.
Record the references you used.
Cross-reference your data.

E. SORT THROUGH YOUR NOTES, IDENTIFYING KEY INFORMATION
and what is missing or what other information you need to know. Organise your information using headings/focus questions.

2. MAKE A PLAN

A. WRITE AN INTRODUCTION
Opening statement: A diamond is forever, or so the television advertisement proclaims… This exquisite gem, the advertisement tells us, represents the promise of enduring love and loyalty.

If these innocuous-looking gems could talk, many would tell tales not of love but of unfathomable violence and destruction – of families torn apart and innocent lives taken, all in the name of profits. Many of the diamonds glinting on fingers, wrists and necklines today are conflict diamonds, also known as blood diamonds.

B. DECIDE ON A LOGICAL ORDER FOR YOUR INFORMATION
What will come first, next…last?

C. WRITE UP YOUR INFORMATION

D. DESIGN SOME VISUALS TO INCLUDE IN YOUR REPORT
You can use graphs, diagrams, labels, charts, tables, cross-sections…

WRITING AN INFORMATIONAL REPORT

Have you...

- recorded important information?
- written in a formal style that is concise and accurate?
- backed up factual statements with credible evidence/details?
- used scientific or technical terms?
- written a logical sequence of facts?
- avoided unnecessary descriptive details, metaphors or similes?
- avoided author bias or opinion?
- evaluated the relevance of your factual content to the topic?

...don't forget to revisit your writing.
Do you need to change, add or delete anything to improve your report?